DEFEND
AND
PROTECT

THE NAVY

Robert Snedden

Gareth Stevens
PUBLISHING

Please visit our website, **www.garethstevens.com**.
For a free color catalog of all our high-quality books,
call toll free 1-800-542-2595 or fax 1-877-542-2596.

Cataloging-in-Publication Data

Snedden, Robert.
The Navy / by Robert Snedden.
p. cm. — (Defend and protect)
Includes index.
ISBN 978-1-4824-4123-9 (pbk.)
ISBN 978-1-4824-4124-6 (6-pack)
ISBN 978-1-4824-4125-3 (library binding)
1. United States. — Navy — Juvenile literature.
2. United States. — Navy — History — Juvenile literature.
3. United States — History, Naval — Juvenile literature.
I. Snedden, Robert. II. Title.
VA58.4 S64 2016
359.00973—d23

First Edition

Published in 2016 by
Gareth Stevens Publishing
111 East 14th Street, Suite 349
New York, NY 10003

© 2016 Gareth Stevens Publishing

Produced by Calcium
Editors: Sarah Eason and Jennifer Sanderson
Designers: Paul Myerscough and Simon Borrough
Picture research: Jennifer Sanderson

Picture credits: Department of Defense (DoD): 22, Chief Petty Officer Ty Swartz 4, John Narewski 23,
Lt. Frederick Martin 13, Lt. j.g. Caleb Swigart 10, Petty Officer 1st Class Carmichael Yepez 34–35, Petty
Officer 1st Class Charles S. Zook 20, Petty Officer 2nd Class Christopher Vickers 36, Petty Officer 2nd
Class Josh Cassatt 18, Petty Officer 2nd Class Kori L. Melvin 17, Petty Officer 2nd Class Kyle D. Gahlau
5, Petty Officer 2nd Class Luke Pinneo 39t, Petty Officer 2nd Class RJ Stratchko 1, 15, Petty Officer 3rd
Class Blake R. Midnight 31, Petty Officer 3rd Class Chris Vickers 45, Petty Officer 3rd Class Randall
Damm 6; Dreamstime: Edvard Molnar 7b, 13b, 17b, 23b, 27b, 31b, 37b, Vudhikrai Sovannakran 5b,
11, 15b, 19, 21, 28b, 34b, 38b, 40b; Shutterstock: Douglas Litchfield 41, Jerry Zitterman 39c, US Army
Spc. Landon Stephenson 7; US Marine Corps Sgt. Esdras Ruano 30; US Navy: 37, John Narewski 28,
Mass Communication Specialist 1st Class Chad Runge 16, Mass Communication Specialist 1st Class Eric
L. Beauregard 42, Mass Communication Specialist 1st Class James Kimber 25, Mass Communication
Specialist 1st Class Steven Myers 27, Mass Communication Specialist 1st Class Talley Reeve 8; US Navy:
Paul Farley 24, Petty Officer 1st Class Terrence Siren 33, Scott A. Thornbloom 14; Wikimedia Commons:
CPOA(Phot) Thomas McDonald 3, 26; LA(Phot) Keith Morgan 43, Scott A. Thornbloom 12.

Printed in the United States of America
CPSIA compliance information: Batch #CW16GS: For further information contact
Gareth Stevens, New York, New York at 1-800-542-2595.

Contents

CHAPTER 1:
Sea Power

The job of a navy is to control and defend the seas around its country's shores, to keep the sea lanes open and safe for merchant ships, and to protect the country's interests overseas. The crew of a navy warship may be called upon to face danger in a hostile environment far from home. It takes courage, skill, and teamwork to do this job. It also requires professionalism and people who take pride in their work.

The guided missile cruiser USS *Shiloh* leads a combined fleet of US and Japanese ships.

Controlling the Seas

The US Navy was first founded in 1775 to take on the might of Britain's Royal Navy, which, at the time, was the most powerful sea force in the world. Today, no other country's navy can match the power and reach of the US Navy's fleets, which sail the seas and oceans of the world, from the Pacific, Atlantic, and Indian Oceans, to the Mediterranean Sea and Persian Gulf.

This book will give you a glimpse of life in the modern navy. You will discover that the navy is about more than just ships at sea. Aircraft carriers, the largest of all warships, can bring a formidable force to attack from the air. Troop transports carry elite marines for an amphibious assault on enemy territory. Submarines prowl like deadly hunters beneath the waves. On shore, dockyards and naval bases provide support for the ships at sea, including equipment maintenance and repair.

Navy SEAL trainees

THINK LIKE A SAILOR

Being a sailor is all about meeting challenges. Sailors test themselves constantly, all the while knowing that they can rely on their team. Whether it is the 30-strong crew of a patrol boat or the thousands that make up a carrier group, sailors learn the strength that comes from working together with others to the best of their abilities.

The Modern Navy

The US Navy is a huge organization with more than 400,000 men and women serving in its ranks. It has nearly 200 combat ships, as well as a number of other support vessels such as minesweepers, patrol craft, and hospital ships.

As well as its ships, a navy also includes a fleet of aircraft that may be stationed on board aircraft carriers or on land. Modern navy combat ships can be divided into seven types: aircraft carriers, cruisers, destroyers, frigates, corvettes, submarines, and amphibious assault ships. Support and auxiliary ships include minesweepers, patrol boats, survey ships, tenders, and oilers.

Aircraft carrier

Units

A navy's forces can be deployed in a variety of units, based on the number of ships involved. For example, the smallest operational unit is just a single ship. Ships may be combined to form squadrons of between three and 10 vessels. A squadron can be made up of just one type of ship or several. In the US Navy, a squadron is usually a formation of destroyers and submarines. A fleet is the largest-sized unit—the equivalent of an army on the land. For a smaller country, a fleet may be its whole navy. A task force is a fleet of ships that has been specially put together to carry out a mission.

The hospital ship USNS *Comfort* sails on a humanitarian mission to Haiti in 2009.

ACT LIKE A TASK FORCE COMMANDER

When Argentina invaded the Falkland Islands in 1982, the British government put together a task force to retake them. The nuclear submarine HMS *Conqueror* was first to set out on April 4, and the aircraft carriers HMS *Invincible* and HMS *Hermes* soon followed. The whole task force eventually totaled 127 ships, including 43 Royal Navy vessels, 22 Royal Fleet auxiliary ships, and 62 merchant ships (including the ocean liners SS *Canberra* and *Queen Elizabeth II*, which were used as troop carriers).

TAKE THE TEST!

Could you be a part of the navy?

Before you join the navy, you need to know a little more about it. How much do you remember about the structure of the navy and its different branches?

Q1. In what year was the US Navy founded?

Q2. How many combat ships are in the US Navy?

Q3. What is the largest type of warship?

Q4. What kind of ships carry marines into combat?

Q5. How many ships make up a squadron?

Q6. What is the navy equivalent of an army?

Q7. Can you name two types of support ship?

Q8. What is the crew size of a patrol boat?

ANSWERS

Q1. 1775
Q2. Nearly 300
Q3. An aircraft carrier
Q4. Troop transports
Q5. Between three and 10 vessels
Q6. A fleet
Q7. Any of the following: minesweeper, patrol boat, survey ship, oiler, or tender
Q8. 30 people

CHAPTER 2: Warships

A navy's ships are built for war at sea. They are fast, tough, and well-armed. Some ships patrol on their own, but others may make up a powerful fleet of many ships centered on an aircraft carrier.

This squadron of guided missile destroyers and cruisers is on a training exercise.

Different ships can be deployed to meet different needs. The carrier provides a wide range of options and is capable of carrying out attacks on enemy targets in the air, on the sea, and ashore. The ships supporting the carrier might include:

★ Guided missile cruisers: these are multi-mission combat ships, equipped with Tomahawk cruise missiles for long-range strike capability.

★ Guided missile destroyers: these multi-mission combat ships are used for antiair warfare.

★ Attack submarines: these seek and destroy enemy ships that threaten the carrier group.

★ Combined ammunition, oiler, and supply ships: these provide the supplies for the carrier group to stay on station and be ready to respond, without having to return to base.

ACT LIKE A CARRIER COMMANDER

On September 11, 2001, the carrier USS *Enterprise* was just beginning her voyage home from the Arabian Gulf to her home port of Norfolk, VA. When the crew saw the live television coverage of the attack on the World Trade Center, the commander of the *Enterprise*, without waiting for orders, headed back to the waters off Southwest Asia. For three weeks, *Enterprise* remained on station, its aircraft flying nearly 700 missions, launching air attacks against al Qaeda terrorist training camps and Taliban military installations in Afghanistan.

Joining the Navy

Enlisted sailors are the workforce of the navy. They hold many different positions and responsibilities across the service.

To join the navy, recruits must meet certain qualifications, such as having a good high school education. They will also have to be ready to commit to serve for a specified amount of time. An enlisted sailor will serve for an initial period of four years or longer.

Before getting on board, new recruits complete eight to 10 weeks of basic training, or boot camp. Once the basic skills have been learned, the recruits begin specialist training for their chosen job aboard a ship. There are hundreds of different roles the new recruits can train for in the navy, from submarine electronics to cyberwarfare engineers, explosive ordinance technicians, and gunners' mates. They can even be navy musicians!

Female US Navy recruits are issued their new uniform.

Physical Readiness Test

All navy trainees have to pass the navy's physical readiness test. The test measures muscle power, endurance, and stamina. It consists of a 1.5-mile (2.4 km) run, sit-ups, and push-ups. A recruit must be able to do more than 50 push-ups in 2 minutes to get a good score. Trainees may also have to do a timed 0.3-mile (0.5 km) swim. Active personnel have to take the test twice a year to prove themselves fit for duty.

Training hard

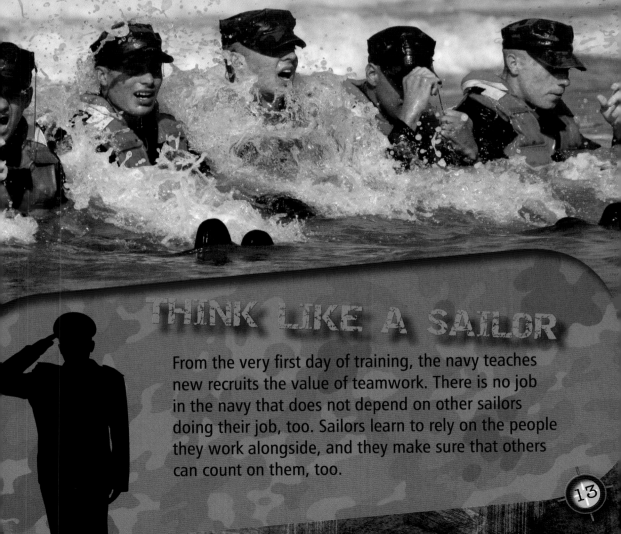

THINK LIKE A SAILOR

From the very first day of training, the navy teaches new recruits the value of teamwork. There is no job in the navy that does not depend on other sailors doing their job, too. Sailors learn to rely on the people they work alongside, and they make sure that others can count on them, too.

Naval Officer

If the enlisted sailors are the workforce of the navy, then the officers might be thought of as its managers and leaders.

Each navy officer is given a rank. Below are some of the ranked positions in the US Navy:

★ **Ensign**: the lowest ranked position, usually taken by graduates of the United States Naval Academy and other training schools. Most are training to specialize in a naval field.

★ **Lieutenant**: a division officer or service head on smaller ships, aircraft squadrons, and submarines

★ **Commander**: can command a frigate, destroyer, fast attack submarine, or aviation squadron

★ **Captain**: commanding officers of aircraft carriers and other major commands

★ **Vice Admiral**: commands fleets and holds a regional command

★ **Admiral**: commands regional commands, joint commands, or is the chief of naval operations

★ **Fleet Admiral**: assigned only during war and has not been assigned since World War II

New naval graduates from the Officer Candidate School look forward to taking up their postings aboard ships.

Warfare Officers

Surface warfare officers are trained to command ships and their crews, directing operations aboard aircraft carriers, cruisers, destroyers, amphibious warfare ships, mine warfare ships, and frigates. The warfare officer is responsible for taking the ship into action, liaising closely with the Operations Room. The outcome of the mission, and the safety of the ship and crew, are in their hands.

Special warfare crewmen

THINK LIKE A WARFARE OFFICER

Surface warfare officers must be prepared for any kind of navy mission. They could find themselves in charge of any number of operations and activities at sea. Their task might be to provide and coordinate air, submarine, and surface ship defense for aircraft carriers in a carrier fleet.

Navy Diver

One of the most specialized and highly skilled professions aboard a ship is that of a navy diver. Intense training prepares divers for everything, from routine ship maintenance and salvage operations to search and rescue, and sabotage.

Dive School

Training to become a navy diver will challenge a recruit's ability and staying power to the maximum. It will test their willpower, intelligence, and physical strength. Diver training is one of the most physically and mentally demanding military training programs. Only the very best and most determined individuals will win through to join this elite band of underwater heroes.

The course begins with seven weeks of training in basic electrical and engineering courses, becoming adapted to long periods in the water, and getting physically fit. This is followed by an additional 15 weeks of training in such things as underwater cutting and welding, ship maintenance, repair and salvage, and laying demolition charges.

A navy diver has to be able to swim 500 yards (457 m) in 12 minutes and 30 seconds, and do 50 push-ups in 2 minutes.

Fully Fledged Divers

When their training is complete, divers will be assigned to a fleet diving unit. There, they will be trained to perform underwater ship repair, salvage, and construction, using either SCUBA equipment or a diving suit. Fleet units also train diving medical officers and technicians.

Divers at work

THINK LIKE A DIVER

The navy divers' motto is "We dive the world over." Members of this elite group of specialists must be prepared to work in just about every undersea environment you could imagine, from icy Arctic conditions and warm tropical seas to sometimes working in deep, murky waters where their tasks have to be completed by touch alone.

Navy Intelligence

As well as possessing formidable firepower, modern navy ships are fitted with state-of-the-art electronics and intelligence-gathering equipment. A successful mission requires knowing as much as possible about what the enemy is doing, while at the same time, making sure they know as little as possible about your plans.

A Combat Direction Center officer aboard the aircraft carrier USS *Ronald Reagan* reviews intelligence information.

Always Alert

Naval intelligence officers play a vital role in national security. They analyze the latest spy reports and interpret images from satellites. They look for patterns of behavior that could alert naval and other military forces to the intentions of an enemy. It is their mission to gain a deep understanding of the enemy's plans. Their intelligence, or intel, can be used to guide the decisions of mission commanders. Intelligence officers can operate aboard ships or at shore bases, depending on their duties.

After first completing officer training, intelligence officers go on a five-month basic course of instruction in electronics, antisubmarine, antisurface, antiair, amphibious and strike warfare, counterintelligence, strategic intelligence, air defense analysis, and combat mission planning. After this, they will go on a 30-month tour of duty aboard an aircraft carrier or amphibious command ship.

ACT LIKE A CYBERWARFARE ENGINEER

Cyberwarfare engineers have to master complex computer networks and the tactical systems they control. They are usually based on shore, for example at a Navy Information Operations Command (NIOC). Cyberwarfare engineers first have to complete officer training before being assigned to their NIOC. There is always the need to learn new skills as computer systems are changing and developing all the time.

TAKE THE TEST!

Could you join the ranks?

What do you know about the role of the navy's surface fleet and some of its important personnel? Take this test to see if you have been paying attention:

Q1. Name two ships you might find in a carrier support group.

Q2. What is the lowest officer rank in the US Navy?

Q3. Within what time should a navy diver be able to swim 500 yards (457 m)?

Q4. How long does the basic training for a new recruit take?

Q5. A cyberwarfare officer is expert in which systems?

Q6. Who is responsible for analyzing spy reports on enemy activities?

Q7. Why did the USS *Enterprise* change course on September 11, 2001?

Q8. Who is responsible for taking a ship into action?

ANSWERS

Q8. The warfare officer.

Q7. They saw the attack on the World Trade Center and went to take station where they would be needed

Q6. The naval intelligence officers

Q5. Computer networks and tactical systems

Q4. Eight to 10 weeks

Q3. 12 minutes and 30 seconds

Q2. Ensign

Q1. Any two of the following: aircraft carrier, guided missile cruiser, attack submarine, supply ship guided missile cruiser, attack submarine, supply ship

CHAPTER 3: Submarines

Patrolling in secret beneath the waves, the submarine fleet keeps watch on the ships and submarines of other nations. Some submarines carry nuclear missiles. These are the ultimate weapons of last resort. Submarines were first widely used during World War I, and today, they form an important part of many navies around the world.

Operating hundreds of feet below the sea, it is absolutely vital that members of a submarine crew know they can rely on each other. This means it is vital to select the right people to serve in the submarine service. Candidates are thoroughly screened for suitability before going through training that may take up to one year. At the end of this, US Navy personnel are allowed to wear the submarine warfare insignia, known as "Earning Your Dolphins."

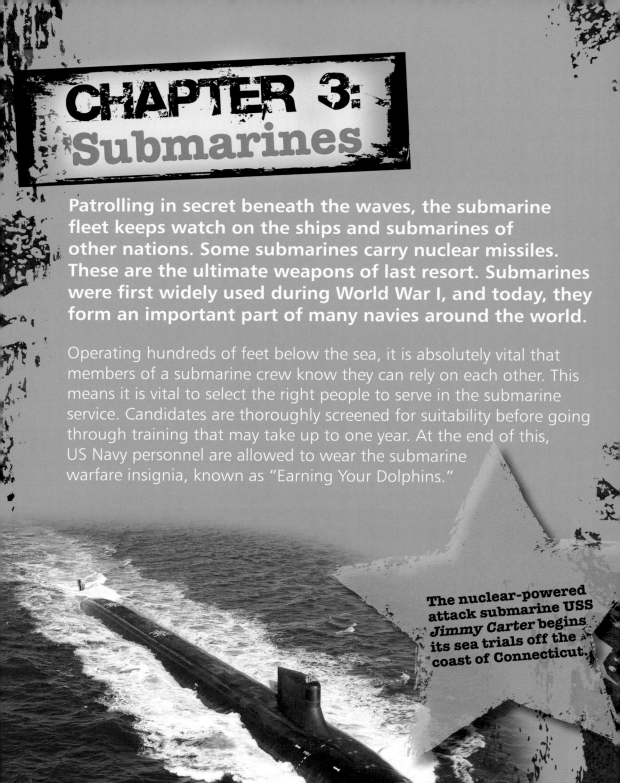

The nuclear-powered attack submarine USS *Jimmy Carter* begins its sea trials off the coast of Connecticut.

Submariners are rotated between sea and shore assignments. A submariner can be on sea duty for a period of three to five years, followed by shore duty for two to three years. Most submarines actually spend a lot of time docked at their home port. On a submarine, the living conditions are confined and there is limited space for onboard supplies, so submarines generally have shorter deployments than surface ships—usually three to six months, depending on the type of boat.

Snow-covered submarine

ACT LIKE A GUIDED MISSILE SUBMARINE COMMANDER

The commander of a guided missile submarine has a formidable weapon at his disposal. Armed with tactical missiles and superior communications, they are equally ready to spy or strike decisively. They are designed to serve and support the needs of special operations forces around the world. Each submarine has a lock-out chamber that allows special operations forces to enter and leave the submarine while it is submerged.

Life Beneath the Sea

Submarines carry fewer crew than most surface ships—typically between 120 and 160 sailors. As the crew is small, each submariner has to be expert in their field, including engineering and weapons. Each sailor must also be skilled in using all of the submarine's systems.

After April 2010, women were allowed to serve aboard US Navy submarines. The first group of female submariners completed their training at nuclear power school and reported on board two ballistic and two guided missile submarines in November 2011. Elsewhere in the US Navy, women make up about 18 percent of the active personnel.

Arriving in port

CHRISTOS XIX
MLS

Submariners practice driving a sub in the dive simulator at the US Navy's Trident Training Facility in Georgia.

Boomers

Ballistic missile submarines—often called "boomers"—are the giants of the submarine fleet. They have a single mission: strategic deterrence. This means discouraging an enemy from attacking by threatening the use of nuclear weapons. They are armed with long-range intercontinental nuclear missiles and patrol the ocean's depths. The US Navy has 14 boomers in operation, each one with enough deadly firepower to make it roughly the fifth-most powerful nation on Earth.

THINK LIKE A SUBMARINER

Submariners might find themselves deep underwater for long periods, perhaps skirting close to enemy territory where the submarine must evade detection. They need to be able to rely on their crewmates, be ready to take on responsibilities at a moment's notice, and react quickly and decisively to emergencies, such as fires or flooding, which could be deadly for the boat and its crew.

Nuclear Submarine Officer

Nuclear submarine officers are responsible for everything that goes into arming and operating a fleet of nuclear submarines. A submarine officer could be driving a vessel, charting its position, overseeing the operation of a nuclear propulsion system, or managing the onboard weapons systems.

To qualify as a nuclear submarine officer, submariners must spend 12 weeks at Officer Candidate School. This is followed by 24 weeks of advanced training at the Naval Nuclear Power School. For the next six months, the submarine officers transfer to the Nuclear Power Training Unit. There, they study the components of an actual nuclear propulsion plant. Successfully completing this training qualifies the officer as an Engineering Officer of the Watch. After this comes the Submarine Officer Basic Course. During this 12-week course, officers learn all about submarine operations, including safety, damage control, seamanship, and the responsibilities of leading a crew of submariners.

The Royal Navy's *HMS Vigilant*

Qualified in Submarines

Shore-based training ends with an assignment as a Division Officer on board a submarine on a three-year tour. This could see submariners out on patrol, in port, and carrying out maintenance. The officers work toward being designated as "Qualified in Submarines," which earns them the right to wear the coveted gold dolphins insignia. After their first sea tour, there is a two-year shore assignment, during which they will pass on their knowledge to new officers at the Nuclear Power Training Unit and Submarine School.

The ultimate goal for many officers will be to one day command their own submarine at sea.

ACT LIKE A REACTORS ENGINEER

Naval reactors engineers are responsible for researching, designing, maintaining, operating, and regulating the nuclear reactors and power plants that drive nuclear submarines and aircraft carriers. It is a challenging role, where the engineer may be in charge of several projects at once, and is one of the most highly respected positions in the navy.

TAKE THE TEST!

Could you be a submariner?

What do you know about submarine warfare and life beneath the surface of the ocean?

Q1. When were submarines first widely used?

Q2. What is it called when a trainee successfully qualifies as a submariner?

Q3. When were women first allowed to serve aboard US Navy submarines?

Q4. How long do officers spend in Nuclear Power School?

Q5. What is the typical crew size of a submarine?

Q6. How long do submarines usually spend on deployment?

Q7. Who is responsible for maintaining the nuclear reactors on a nuclear submarine?

Q8. What are ballistic missile submarines sometimes called?

ANSWERS

Q8. Boomers
Q7. Naval reactors engineers
Q6. Three to six months
Q5. 120 to 160 sailors
Q4. 24 weeks
Q3. After April 2010
Q2. Earning Your Dolphins
Q1. During World War I

Naval infantry, commonly known as marines, carry out missions on land and at sea, including boarding enemy vessels and amphibious landings on enemy territory. They also take part in land warfare, acting separately from naval operations.

The marines are ready to deploy anywhere in the world, using the navy to get them where they need to be. The training to become a marine is long and tough, and only the most able recruits will make it through. In most countries, the marine force is part of the navy, but the US Marine Corps is a separate armed service in its own right, with its own leadership structure.

Marine Corps training is designed to give each marine the confidence, determination, and physical strength and fitness to succeed and survive in any combat situation.

Navy SEALs

The US Navy's Sea, Air, and Land Forces—known as SEALs—are one of the world's most elite groups, ready to take on counterterrorism and reconnaissance missions deep in enemy territory. SEALs are trained to a very high standard of physical fitness and operate in small units. They have to think fast, have huge reserves of willpower, and be focused on the success of their mission.

SEAL training has been described as brutal. The 12 months of initial training, which includes Basic Underwater Demolition School and Parachute Jump School, is followed by 18 months of predeployment training and specialized training.

Navy SEALs

ACT LIKE A NAVY SEAL

Navy SEALs have to be prepared to reach their objective by any means, including parachute, submarine, helicopter, high-speed boat, foot patrol, or by a combat swimmer insertion. They are trained to operate in any environment, including urban areas, mountains, jungles, and deserts.

Navy Pilot

Navy pilots and flight officers are a vital part of the navy's combat team. Pilots may be called upon to collect photographic intelligence on enemy movements, carry out attacks on enemy forces, take part in antisubmarine warfare, or carry out search-and-rescue operations.

Flight officers train in aircraft engine systems, the use of electronic countermeasures, navigation, weather forecasting, and flight planning. To be accepted onto the navy pilot course, candidates must be college graduates who have also completed officer training. At flight school, pilots and flight officers do their flight and navigation training, eventually focusing on specific missions and aircraft types.

Blue Angels

Navy and Marine Corps jet pilots with an aircraft carrier qualification and a minimum of 1,250 tactical jet flight-hours, are eligible to try out for the Blue Angels. The Blue Angels are the US Navy's flight demonstration squadron of F/A-18 Hornets. A total of 16 officers voluntarily serve with the Blue Angels. The Chief of Naval Air Training selects the "Boss," the Blue Angels Commanding Officer, who flies jet Number 1. The Boss must have at least 3,000 tactical jet flight-hours and have commanded a tactical jet squadron.

The skilled pilots of the Blue Angels fly in a tight formation during a training flight over the beaches of Florida.

ACT LIKE A BLUE ANGEL

Selection for the Blue Angels is based on professional ability, military bearing, and communication skills. During training, the pilots fly 120 missions in two practice sessions a day, six days a week, to ensure that they will perform the demonstration safely and flawlessly.

TAKE THE TEST!

Could you survive on land and in the air?

What do you know about the navy's ability to fight on land and in the air? Take the test!

Q1. What are the naval infantry commonly known as?

Q2. What does SEAL stand for?

Q3. Who trains at the Basic Underwater Demolition School?

Q4. In which environments are Navy SEALs trained to operate?

Q5. How many training missions do the Blue Angels fly?

Q6. Is the US Marine Corps part of the Navy?

Q7. Name two things flight officers train in.

Q8. What kind of aircraft do the Blue Angels fly?

ANSWERS

Q8. F/A-18 Hornets

Q7. Any two of the following: aircraft engine systems, electronic countermeasures, navigation, weather forecasting, and flight planning

Q6. No, it is a separate armed service in its own right

Q5. 120

Q4. Any environment

Q3. Navy SEALs

Q2. Sea, Air, and Land Forces

Q1. Marines

A naval base is where ships are stationed when they have no active mission. At the ship's home port, the vessel can be resupplied and maintenance can be carried out. The US Naval Facilities Engineering Command is responsible for the planning, design, and construction of shore facilities, for US Navy activities around the world. It provides the Navy with the operating, support, and training bases it needs.

A naval base is a tight-knit community. The base is like a town with everything, from grocery stores and hospitals to police and fire departments. Often, there is a movie theater and library, too.

The aircraft carrier USS *George Washington* leaves Naval Station Norfolk as it sets out on a new deployment.

Naval Station Norfolk

The world's largest naval base is Naval Station Norfolk in Virginia, which is home to the Atlantic Fleet. It has responsibility for operations in the Atlantic and Indian Oceans and the Mediterranean Sea. It is the home port for 5 carriers and 7 submarines, as well as a number of other vessels. It has 14 piers that can allow 75 ships to dock at any one time. There are also 11 hangers for more than 130 aircraft. Every year, more than 3,000 ships enter or leave the base, and more than 250 flights are made from the base every day.

ACT LIKE AN IN-PORT OFFICER

The in-port officer of the deck (OOD) is one of the most important people on the ship, along with the captain and the executive officer, with all the authority of command. The in-port OOD supervises and inspects onboard activities while in port, and is always ready to respond quickly. Security of the ship is one of the most important duties of the in-port OOD. The OOD is always mindful of the weather when the ship is anchored, moored, or secured to a pier.

US Naval Base Guam

Coast Guard Patrol

Depending on the country, the coast guard may be a branch of the military in its own right, a part of the navy, or a completely civilian organization. The responsibilities of the coast guard vary from country to country. Some coast guards are heavily armed military forces, imposing customs and maintaining coastal security. Others may be volunteer groups with no law enforcement powers, whose role it is to carry out search-and-rescue missions offshore.

In peacetime, the US Coast Guard (USCG) is a branch of the military in its own right, distinct from the navy. It is responsible for keeping ports secure, performing rescue missions, ensuring the safety of commercial shipping around the coast, and protecting the ocean environment. Nearly 42,000 men and women are currently in active service in the USCG.

Boatswain's Mates

Boatswain's mates (BMs) can be found serving on every US Coast Guard vessel, from harbor tugs to the latest National Security Cutters. BMs are capable of performing almost any task to do with the operation of their boat, as well as supervising the boat's deck personnel and the supporting shore unit. BMs load cargo using hoists and winches and know about the different uses of ropes and cables. They take charge of security details, navigation, and communication, and will conduct search-and-rescue and law-enforcement operations. BMs can become officers-in-charge of patrol boats, river tenders, harbor tugs, or search-and-rescue stations onshore.

Coast Guard officers take part in cold water survival training in Boston Harbor.

A rescue diver goes to work

ACT LIKE A COAST GUARD

It takes courage and determination to be a coast guard. Members of the coast guard may be called upon to put their own lives at risk, rescuing others in hazardous conditions. They may have to confront dangerous drug smugglers or bring polluters to justice. Their training gives them the skills and confidence to carry out these tasks.

TAKE THE TEST!

Could you be an onshore officer?

Do you remember enough to pass the training to be an onshore officer?

Q1. What is a ship's home port?

Q2. What is the world's largest naval base?

Q3. Which organization is responsible for planning naval shore facilities?

Q4. How many ships can dock in Naval Station Norfolk at any one time?

Q5. How many personnel are currently active in the US Coast Guard?

Q6. Who is responsible for protecting the marine environment—the US Navy or the US Coast Guard?

Q7. Who is responsible for supervising the deck crew on a Coast Guard Cutter?

Q8. Which fleet is based at Naval Station Norfolk?

ANSWERS

Q8. The Atlantic Fleet
Q7. The boatswain's mate
Q6. The US Coast Guard
Q5. Nearly 42,000
Q4. 75 ships
Q3. The US Naval Facilities Engineering Command
Q2. Naval Station Norfolk
Q1. The place where it is based when not deployed or on patrol

CHAPTER 6:
Working Together

Ships from the navies of different countries sometimes join forces to accomplish a mission. Combined Maritime Forces (CMFs) is a naval partnership between several countries that aims to combat terrorism, prevent piracy, and keep the oceans safe for shipping. The CMF also offers aid to the victims of natural disasters.

The CMF is commanded by a US Navy vice admiral and is based at US Naval Support Activity Bahrain. It is made up of three main combined task forces (CTFs):

A team from part of CTF-151 captures a group of Somali pirates.

★ CTF-150: responsible for security and counterterrorism

★ CTF-151: responsible for counterpiracy

★ CTF-152: ensures Arabian Gulf security

CTF-150

CTF-150's area of operation (AOR) spans the Red Sea, Gulf of Aden, Indian Ocean, and Gulf of Oman. The safety of this area is vital for world trade because it includes the main shipping routes from the Far East to Europe and the United States.

Destroyer from CT-150

ACT LIKE A CTF MEMBER

On April 8, 2009, four Somali pirates took control of the US-flagged container ship *Maersk Alabama*. The crew members put up a fight and the pirates fled in one of the ship's lifeboats, taking Captain Richard Phillips captive. Fortunately for Phillips, ships of CTF-151 were nearby. The destroyer USS *Bainbridge* was the first to respond and reached the lifeboat on the night of April 9. The destroyer used spotlights, loudspeakers, and sirens to keep the pirates on edge while they awaited the arrival of SEAL Team 6, flying in from Virginia to make the rescue. Under cover of darkness, the SEALs parachuted into the ocean and climbed aboard the *Bainbridge*. From the deck of the ship, the SEALs used sniper fire to kill the pirates and set Phillips free, unharmed.

43

Have You Got What It Takes?

If you want to join the US Navy, following these steps is a good place to start:

School

A good education is vital. You will need at least a high school diploma to enlist in the navy. If you aim to serve as an officer, a college education is essential. Shipmates are always sharing their knowledge with each other. Be willing and ready to go further than school lessons—read and learn for yourself and have an inquiring mind.

Join a Team

Teamwork is everything in the navy. The navy is no place for a loner. Join a group, whether it is a sports team or a voluntary group, and develop your team skills.

Learn Another Language

More than any other service, the navy travels the world to distant ports of call. Language skills will help you communicate with local people.

Fitness

Remember, you need to be able to do 50 push-ups to get a good grade at boot camp. Join a sports team to keep you physically fit.

Be Disciplined

If you start a task, see it through to the best of your abilities.

Glossary

aircraft carrier a large warship from which aircraft can take off and land

amphibious able to operate on land or sea

ballistic missile short for intercontinental ballistic missile (ICBM), a missile with a range of more than 3,400 miles (5,472 km)

boot camp a training camp for new recruits

cutter a light, fast coastal patrol boat

cyber to do with computers and information technology

deployment moving forces into a position of readiness

deterrence having enough firepower to make an enemy too scared to start a war

enlisted to have joined one of the armed services

home port the port where a ship has its base

hostile unfriendly

merchant ship a civilian ship carrying passengers or cargo

minesweeper a ship equipped to detect and remove explosive mines

oiler a ship carrying fuel oil for other ships

reactor a device that produces energy from nuclear reactions

reconnaissance observing an area to determine enemy activity

sabotage to deliberately destroy something

salvage to rescue a disabled ship and its cargo

SCUBA short for self-contained underwater breathing apparatus, equipment used for diving

squadron a group of warships

strategic long-term military objectives

tactical actions planned to gain a military advantage

task force an armed force organized to carry out a particular objective

For More Information

Books

Greve, Tom. *US Navy: Naval Power* (Freedom Forces).
Vero Beach, FL: Rourke Educational Media, 2013.

Jackson, Kay. *Navy Ships in Action* (Amazing Military Vehicles).
New York, NY: PowerKids Press, 2009.

Leavitt, Amie Jane. *US Navy by the Numbers* (Military by
the Numbers). Mankato, MN: Capstone Press, 2014.

Nagel, Jeanne. *Navy* (US Military Forces). New York, NY:
Gareth Stevens Publishing, 2011.

Websites

Find out more about the US Navy at:
www.navy.com/navy.html

Everything you need to know about joining the military is at:
www.todaysmilitary.com/joining

Learn about the US Navy SEALs at:
www.navyseals.com/nsw/learn-about-the-us-navy-seals

Publisher's note to educators and parents: Our editors have carefully reviewed these
web sites to ensure that they are suitable for students. Many web sites change
frequently, however, and we cannot guarantee that a site's future contents will
continue to meet our high standards of quality and educational value. Be advised
that students should be closely supervised whenever they access the Internet.

Index